ABC USA

Library of Congress Cataloging-in-Publication Data Available

4 6 8 10 9 7 5 3

Published by Sterling Publishing Co., Inc.
387 Park Avenue South, New York, NY 10016
© 2005 by Martin Jarrie
Distributed in Canada by Sterling Publishing
C/o Canadian Manda Group, 165 Dufferin Street,
Toronto, Ontario, Canada M6K 3H6
Distributed in Great Britain and Europe by Chris Lloyd at Orca Book
Services, Stanley House, Fleets Lane, Poole BH15 3AJ, England
Distributed in Australia by Capricorn Link (Australia) Pty. Ltd.
P.O. Box 704, Windsor, NSW 2756, Australia

Printed in China

Sterling ISBN 1-4027-1619-2

For information about custom editions, special sales, premium and
corporate purchases,please contact Sterling Special Sales
Department at 800-805-5489 or specialsales@sterlingpub.com.

ABC USA

Illustrated by
MARTIN JARRIE

Sterling Publishing Co., Inc.
New York

A is for alligator

B is for baseball

C is for cars

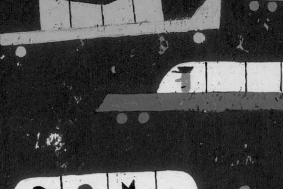

D is for the Declaration
of Independence

E is for the Empire State Building

F is for flag

G is for the Grand Canyon

H is for Hollywood

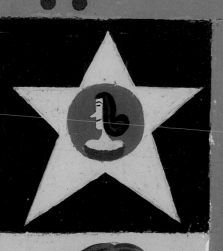

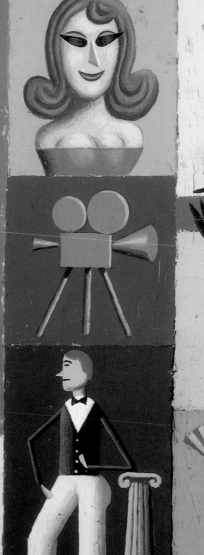

I is for immigrants

K is for the Kentucky Derby

L is for the Liberty Bell

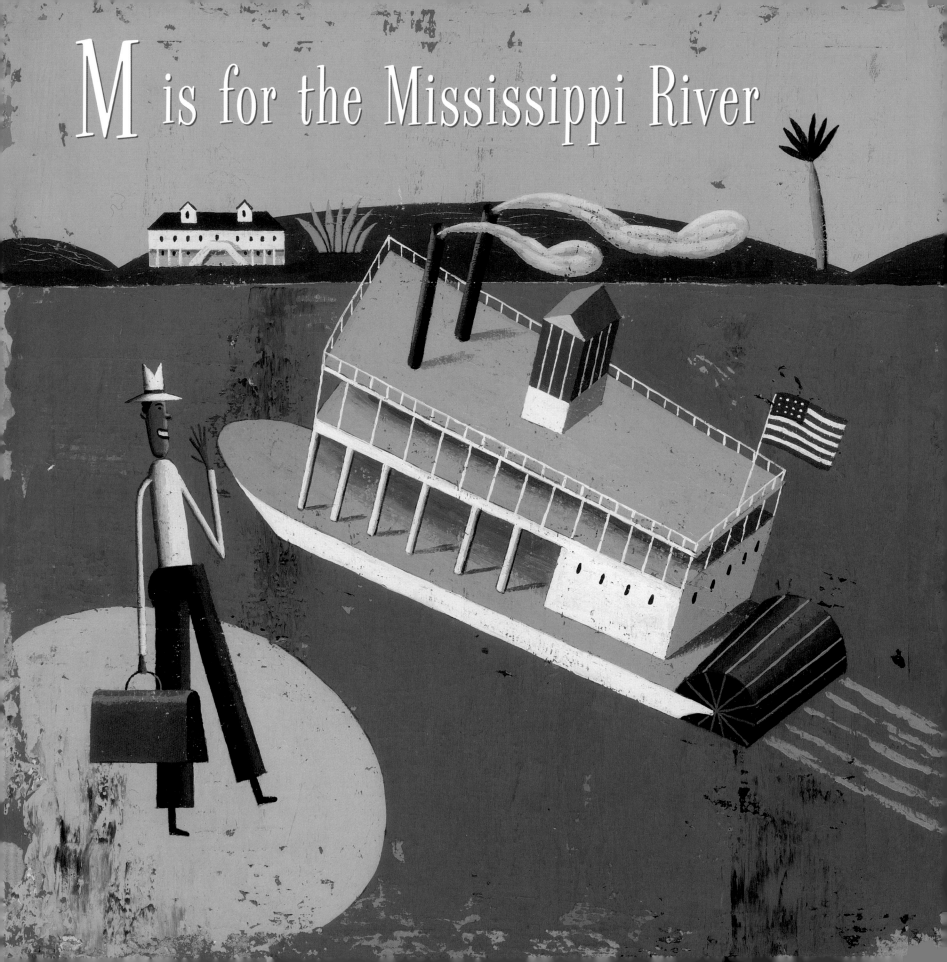

M is for the Mississippi River

N is for Navajo

O is for oranges

P is for pilgrims

Q is for quilts

R is for rodeo

S is for the Smoky Mountains

U is for the Underground Railroad

V is for Valley Forge

W is for the White House

X is for X-roads

Y is for
Yellowstone
National Park

Z is for Zydeco

ALPHABET GLOSSARY

A  The American **alligator** is the largest reptile in North America, ranging in size from 13 to 18 feet long. In 1967, the alligator was placed on the endangered species list and in 1987 it was named the official state reptile of Florida.

B  Since its appearance in the early 1800s, **baseball** has come to be known as the national pastime of the United States. The first baseball stadium, Forbes Field in Pittsburgh, was not constructed until 1909, over 100 years after baseball began in America.

C  The introduction of **cars** to the United States in the early 1900s led to the growth of suburbs and the development of an elaborate system of highways. Increased demand for cars and the need to produce them quickly resulted in the invention of the assembly line by Henry Ford.

D  On July 4, 1776, Thomas Jefferson completed the **Declaration of Independence**, which stated the rights of the American people to "life, liberty, and the pursuit of happiness," and declared the American colonies independent of British rule.

E  Constructed during the Great Depression, The **Empire State Building** was the result of a competition between the founders of Chrysler and General Motors to see who could build the tallest building first. At 102 stories, it was the world's tallest building for 41 years.

F  The first American **flag**, sewn by Betsy Ross in May of 1776, displayed only 13 stars. Today the flag has 50 stars, one per state, and has 13 stripes to symbolize the 13 original colonies.

G 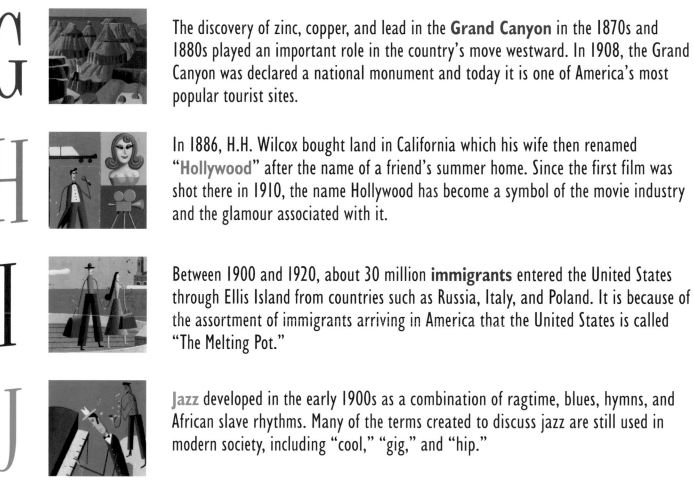 The discovery of zinc, copper, and lead in the **Grand Canyon** in the 1870s and 1880s played an important role in the country's move westward. In 1908, the Grand Canyon was declared a national monument and today it is one of America's most popular tourist sites.

H In 1886, H.H. Wilcox bought land in California which his wife then renamed "**Hollywood**" after the name of a friend's summer home. Since the first film was shot there in 1910, the name Hollywood has become a symbol of the movie industry and the glamour associated with it.

I Between 1900 and 1920, about 30 million **immigrants** entered the United States through Ellis Island from countries such as Russia, Italy, and Poland. It is because of the assortment of immigrants arriving in America that the United States is called "The Melting Pot."

J **Jazz** developed in the early 1900s as a combination of ragtime, blues, hymns, and African slave rhythms. Many of the terms created to discuss jazz are still used in modern society, including "cool," "gig," and "hip."

K 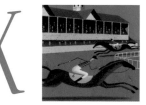 The **Kentucky Derby** was established in 1875 as part of a weeklong celebration of local southern culture. Today the derby is the first of three races that make up horse racing's Triple Crown, and is one of the most prestigious and recognized sporting events in the country.

L  The **Liberty Bell** was first rung on July 8, 1776, following the first public reading of the Declaration of Independence. The large crack in the bell occurred in 1835 when it was rung to observe the death of Supreme Court Chief Justice John Marshall.

M

During America's early years, the **Mississippi River** played a central role in the exploration and financial development of the country. Today, due in large part to the writings of Mark Twain, the river is recognized as the symbol of America's spirit and individuality.

N

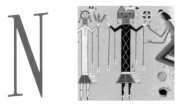

During World War II, a large group of **Navajo** Indians, known as Navajo Code Talkers, assisted the United States by joining the armed forces and developing a method of communication based on their native language that the Japanese were unable to decipher.

O

Oranges, which originated in China, have been growing in Florida since the 16th century. In 2003, almost 1.5 million gallons of Florida orange juice were consumed in the United States.

P

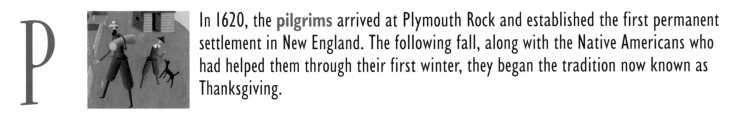

In 1620, the **pilgrims** arrived at Plymouth Rock and established the first permanent settlement in New England. The following fall, along with the Native Americans who had helped them through their first winter, they began the tradition now known as Thanksgiving.

Q

In the 1800s, women used **quilts** to express their political opinions. During the Civil War, these opinions were expressed through "underground railroad quilts," which were hung in the windows of houses where slaves could safely hide as they made their way to freedom.

R

One of America's original sports, the **rodeo** became a popular form of entertainment in the late 1800s. Today it is one of the few remaining symbols of the Old West and the American frontier.

S

The **Smoky Mountains**, the oldest range of mountains in the world, are named for the smoke-like haze that surrounds them. Today the mountain range is the most popular national park in America.

T

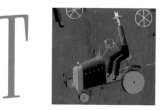

The invention of the **tractor** changed farming in America by providing farmers with a way to more efficiently produce their crops. Today the tractor reminds us of the fading family farms that once populated the country.

U

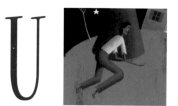

The **Underground Railroad** was a network of escape routes through which anti-slavery northerners illegally helped slaves reach free states and Canada. The publicity surrounding escaped slaves played a crucial role in the events leading up to the Civil War.

V

In December of 1777, General George Washington and his troops made their winter camp at **Valley Forge** in Pennsylvania. This time, during which many of Washington's men died of cold and starvation, is remembered as one of the darkest periods of the American Revolution.

W

Originally a nickname, the term **White House** became official in 1901 when President Theodore Roosevelt had the name engraved on his stationery. With the exception of George Washington, during whose presidency it was built, every US president has resided in the White House.

X

The term crossroads (**"X-roads"**) refers to the crossroads of highways 49 and 61 in the Mississippi Delta. Legend claims that at this crossroads blues musician Robert Johnson sold his soul to the devil in exchange for musical greatness.

Y

Established in 1872, **Yellowstone National Park** was the world's first national park. Yellowstone is also the home of the world's most famous geyser, Old Faithful, which erupts for up to 5 minutes every 30 to 90 minutes.

Z

Zydeco, a uniquely American style of music, originated with the African American creoles of Louisiana and contains elements of jazz, blues, country and western, and traditional Cajun music. The most important instrument in zydeco music is the piano accordion.

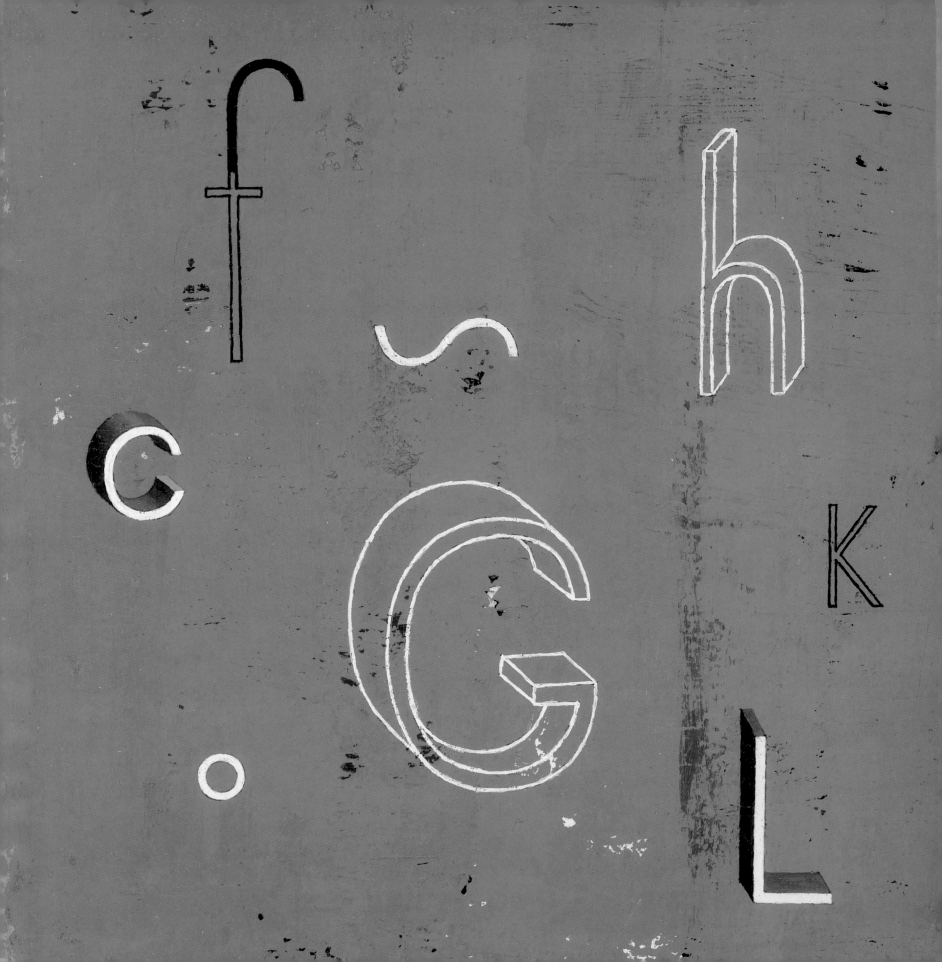